LILIES
of LIFE

LILIES of LIFE

NATASA CUC TO

ReadersMagnet, LLC

Lilies of Life
Copyright © 2023 by Natasa Cuc To

Published in the United States of America
ISBN   Paperback: 978-1-960629-55-5
ISBN   eBook: 978-1-960629-21-0

All rights reserved. No part of this publication may be reproduced, stored in a retrieval system or transmitted in any way by any means, electronic, mechanical, photocopy, recording or otherwise without the prior permission of the author except as provided by USA copyright law.

The opinions expressed by the author are not necessarily those of ReadersMagnet, LLC.

ReadersMagnet, LLC
10620 Treena Street, Suite 230 | San Diego, California, 92131 USA
1.619. 354. 2643 | www.readersmagnet.com

Book design copyright © 2023 by ReadersMagnet, LLC. All rights reserved.

Cover design by Ericka Obando
Interior design by Dorothy Lee

TABLE OF CONTENTS

Morning Love 11

Enticing Love - Adult Content 12

Our Love Dream 14

Magical Moment 15

Lily 16

Nature With Love 17

Our Love - (Adult Content) 18

Lover 19

Lover - (Adult Content) 20

Love Moment 21

Joy - (Adult Content) 22

Soul Of The Poet 23

Sufferer 24

Our Souvenirs - (Adult Content) 25

Our Spring 26

Summer Love 27

Spring Without You 28

The Lover 29

The Spring Moment 30

Love You 31

Feeling Love 32

The Fresh Air To Love 33

The Lovely Fall 34

Morning Summer 35

The High School	36
Saigon City	37
Ten	38
His Arms	39
Teenager	40
The Young Girl, An Angel Friend	41
Doctors	43
My Inspirational Poets	44
Handsome Lover	45
Afternoon Autumn's Love	46
World Now	47
Happiness	48
Feeling Lost	49
Her Family	51
Secret Love	52
My Inspiration	53
I Traveled With Love	54
"So Much Within Me…"	55
Dear Mom	56
Souvenirs	57
Springtime	58
That Summer Moments	59
When Summer Comes	60
The Heroes	61
Red	63
At Moment	64
Dream	65
Autumn Pleasure	66
Generation 6/13/2007	68
One More Time	69
The Dream Come Along Well	70

Him My Sunshine 71

Closed Friends 72

River 73

A Friend Is The Desire Ocean — 74

Her Songs At Key West 76

Nature 78

Love Life As My Soul 79

A Summer Day 80

A Sweet Kiss 81

Tomatoes 82

Loneliness Love 83

Still I Love 84

Kiss Of My Desire Ocean 86

A Love Song 87

Missing Colors 88

Afternoon Love 89

Amanda Hartley 90

Autumn At Virginia 91

Broken Heart' 92

Missing Love 93

Conscious Mind 94

Moonlight- Haiku 95

Mom And I 96

Him... 97

Mom And Buddha 98

I Lost Mom'S Love 99

INTRODUCTION

Dear readers

There's an imagination to write all the poems that I chose to publish in this book. I do hope that all the readers will enjoy my poems.

I make the poems by an imagination and the deep moments stir within me as an event, the beautiful scene or the history event act.

My real career is in being a Software Professional. I do not have any background in literature or writing the poems.

I start to write the poem since 2001. My first convention was Los Angeles on 2001 and my new poem called "love life" was published at that time. Lot of my poems were written and published at the website called www.poetry.com as I received a lot of awards there.

Beyond my pleasure of writing poems. I do hope to be at the service of all my readers and do accept all of the comments as I think of learning the good way to be served the readers and to improve my writing of the poems. While it may not be possible to achieve the magical moment in all my poems. My literary life is affected by the poets around the world.

I have always been greatly impressed and influenced by the poets around the world. Most of my poems that I wrote by an imagination, reading the books, or a history event act.

As the reader can see in the below poem called "My inspiration"
My Inspiration

Blessing with the poets, and eternal joy,
who gave me spirits loves, and spirits care.
The poets, who on world have made me inspires
of truth and pure love by heavenly gate!
Oh, may be my name be poet among poet's world,
then happily would I end my desire days.

My second career as poet makes me love people a lot as I read all the poems at website www.poemhunter.com to learn and to inspire the poets. Learning by myself paying a lot of respects to the poets the entire world. My education at University of Maryland as Bachelor Of Science at College Park at Maryland. My childhood was at Saigon South Vietnam. I love to reside long at Fairfax county and Prince William county (USA). There's take a lot of time to write my poems without any one support where I love to make the poems by self learning.

Finally I do hope all the readers will love my poems and do appreciate them to take time to read my poems.

My first poem book is dedicated to my mom "LANG NGUYEN". Who encourages me to read the poems for her while she is on her wheel chair? I also want to dedicate my first book to my friend Tommy Gerald. I do hope the first book of my poem will be the pleasure for all the readers as well as all my poet's friends at website called www.poemhunter.com. Again I would like to say all my thanks to all the professors at all the conventions that I learned and having the lectures with them.

The Lord is near. Have no anxiety, but in every prayer and supplication with Thanksgiving

Let your petitions be made known to God._Philippians

MORNING LOVE

---·♦·---

The brightest sunshine morning as I can see.
The bluebirds start to sing morning love song.
Flowers bloom everywhere of springtime›s.
We walk through beautiful scenes of the blue morning;
The sun is so bright,
a gentle breeze stirs our desires;
Your eyes are so lovely and so warm.
I fall in love with YOU
For the special morning love in time.

ENTICING LOVE - ADULT CONTENT

Sweet thoughts
With your skin on my skin.
A burned desire traps my soul
You whisper on my ears
with your lips
Perfectly close
my face.
Enticing the love
Perfect moment in time.
You dance
And I stand nearby
perfectly fitting
Or am I dream of?
A marvelous undefined
the feeling you proceed.
Moving you insides
touching my body
Where the voice of pleasure start to moan.
Inexplicable sensations
I welcome you inside
that leave me wanting

More and more making love.
Give me more and more
Of your touch.
I consume every bit of your love.
Hungrily reach to the end
And love you as my young desires.

OUR LOVE DREAM

Quiet as the blue sky
Another beautiful moment passed by
Allowing a rainbow gleam that entire dream
to tenderness kiss the night stars awake.
Once our special moment together
we hold for hands in hands
Two lovers in spring's eve
this harvest of our romance love
Has sustained you and I
Over many moments fascinating evening
our pleasure we long remember
For this special moment in time
Till it captures our lover's dream together.

MAGICAL MOMENT

I stand next to you of the spring
starting to know
We apart or together
we are on the spring.
Sharing in sweetness of love,
disregarding fears of farewell.
I would like you hold me tight
My heart beats wanting you to make me
whole
As my soul merges on blue sky,
pleasure from your kiss, love making.
Let me love deep inside of you
Let me love you, forget our teardrops
Let me love you with my whole heart
As I remember that magical moment
will always be a wonderful life never forget.

LILY

Lilies are so tenderness and full desires of love
within your soul
As you're soft and I am emotive with sense of love.
The feelings of lilies to be found within
Did through the spring
now the blue sky invites me
To the spring of lilies
I am rejoicing of the eternity everywhere.
Lilies are so beautiful,
sweet fragrance lilies fill our souls with joy.

NATURE WITH LOVE

Sunshine,
of spring
the flowers,
of lilies leaves.
Bluebirds sweet,
and bumblebees,
the softest smiles,
sing a song.
A laugh,
a kiss,
the squirrels wander,
tender love with you,
whisper on my ears.
All nature's perfect,
Is in heaven's gate
for I am going
To spend my life with you.

OUR LOVE - (ADULT CONTENT)

Every night I watch the blue sky.
Of you and me in the love boat.
Pass the moment of moments
to think of the lovely scenes
Suddenly appear at the end of the rainbow.
And feeling of your warmth hands hold in mine.
Such tenderness of you that touch.
We kiss each other at somewhere nobody around.
Just you and I fall in with love.
As always the sweet love we got.

LOVER

I do not know what I will
say to my lover.
With my whole heart
for the moments only be
With you.
Loving you is so hard.
Will it never die?
Or am I dream of him?
So may be after all I loved.
My heart it cries each night.
Wanting you make me whole again.
For only when I am with you.
Tears still come easily.
Even after all you
Would not hurt me in some way.

LOVER - (ADULT CONTENT)

You thought of me as lover.
Wanting to touch me if I want to.
Biting my breasts with the tender's love.
Kissing me a lot of time,
undressing and showing me the true love.
Watching me as you believe me as lover,
taking me to the blue skies.
The place where my soul spins,
my body is hot and out of control.
All feelings are beyond the heaven's gate
there were many wonderful moments
That I look ahead for the wonderful man
And found myself the love so beautiful and so marvelous.
To be your lover that I
Always want to and having the highly desire in mine.

LOVE MOMENT

The flowers are blooming
To let you know spring are coming.
My love comes from the spring
With sunshine, sky and cloud that
invite me, welcome you.
I look into your eyes
That leaving me a feeling of love.
Tenderness you touch my cheek.
My soul is aroused as you taste
my mouth, my hands and my heart.
Kiss me soft, sweetly and undress me.
All the love moments fill me with pleasure.
Wonder if you are in my dream
that draw my soul into yours.

JOY - (ADULT CONTENT)

When I thought of him as
The smiles, the beliefs and fascinations
leaded me with all the lovely desires.
My joy for him is never ending.
AS his black eyes
Drawing me like willing person
to give all his wants:
As he touches, gives me a kiss.
The joy starts to grow for the special times.
An admiration connected the desires
To be with him the special moments in time.
So wonderful and so marvelous.
My joy for him beholds, so strong
and so forever.

SOUL OF THE POET

———•———

Soul of our souls sinks in the glass wine
where all poems in that glass wine
Exists-one only; an assured love
that the procession of our fate
Which my life holds, they readily may conceive
whoever stood to watch mountains?
In some still touch the moon of they're own, and seen,
within the deep of its capacious breast,
thought trees, rocks, clouds, and blue sky;
and, On its glassy surface, our souls of foam
Numerous as stars; that our souls on the sky
Beloved to see the emotion of the stars,
Else impossible to know.
08-01-2006

SUFFERER

My friend! Enough to talk you have given.
The purpose of hating asks no more:
Nor more would she have talked as due to one:
Who, in her worst love life, had broken heart?
The unbounded might of prayer; and love, with soul
Fixed on the Buddha status, that consolation springs,
from stirring deeper far than deepest pain,
for the seek sufferer

OUR SOUVENIRS - (ADULT CONTENT)

At last moment that I see you
your eyes make my heart beating fast
Your smile warms up my soul.
I walk with you under great sunshine
to let you know we fall in with love
We not start our life yet,
but your sweet love still exists in me.
I long remember we were on the beautiful
place at Japan and walked in the hallway full Orchids.
Japan made us having the marvelous moments
Oh, my lover!
I wish I can come back to Japan that
we nourish our sweet souvenirs
To wish our souvenirs always brighten our love life
and I would say: "Darling, C'est ma vie"

OUR SPRING

Spring, when our steps walk through the golden flowers
your hands hold in mine
When we deep stir in wonderful moments
Forgetting to live the blossom April,
covering rainbow and wipe me up the teardrops
when we are happy
Our thoughts fly to the sky
Add true love in my soul
And wrap me up with your love.
AS if the weather allows us the perfect time to
rejoice the sweet harmony.

SUMMER LOVE

That summer moment exists,
thinking of the gleam of all my dreams.
I feel you / I sing the love song.
Every days and nights are the happy days
The love moment of that hot summer
keeping me alive
As our love sink in happiness
and our life
Heading to new love
As if weather permits to
See you again.
A chance to live with joy,
to let his arms hold me tight
In that summer perfect in time.
Oh! My goodness,
I wish my love life
Will never ending
And my love for you
Will be forever and always

SPRING WITHOUT YOU

You left me that morning fall.
The white butterfly was sad.
Making the colored flowers fall fast.
AS I sat next to your guitar.
Till the autumn passed by, winter came to an end.
All the melodies… flow over the spring.
Sunglow and rain are on the cloudy sky.
Because you left me, the sky starts rain.
Watching the spring… missing you.
The grass is still green.
Having his absence.
And the sunshine is multicolored.
People fall in love with.
The spring of the evening,
sending to him the red roses.
Happy New Spring…
I only know: loving you.

THE LOVER

Like the beautiful blue star,
admired by the morning sunshine,
the bluebirds sing love song.
Since, We touch each other.
Dreaming of the moonlight with colors.
Reaching out to the roses of my garden:
Red, yellow, pink, a sight only in love.
Beautiful roses bloom everywhere.
So much love of the colored roses.
Across open door, we talk.
Golden flowers forever locked inside.
An erotic dream comes true.
Our love like the huge pacific sea
All I will forever love in my life is my lover.

THE SPRING MOMENT

Colorful Spring flowers
unconcerned with your smiles
Freely blow your eyes
soft caresses in the dark
I hear the beating of your heart
with a kiss, the fire starts
As passions of moments pass by
your breath burns hot
My teardrops are on my face
I feel my body shaking
A moon appears somewhere on the sky
the feel of our souls melt into one.
Smell the refreshing warmth of the cool spring moment.

LOVE YOU

Walking the long way in the bright light,
here my friends comes in the house,
I watch him pull and push the front door so heavy, brown, old,
new so lovely world, sound and songs are so marvelous.
We hands in hands, then kiss.
I feel his entire body-weight on my body,
His mouth is on my mouth, pulling me toward new life.
The gleaming of my dreams and he loves
With lot of the touch in our souls.
We become friendship in that lovely within the second.
The lovely time is gone with embrace and
Continue like the delicious love.
When he is gone for several months.
His touch is still strong in mine.
My love desire is in me longer
From his love for me deep into the rainbow.
I must accept it like the soft love
That his soft hands, his black eyes,
The miracle of him, and of the heaven's gate itself,
making me fall in with him that he never knows
My secret love.

FEELING LOVE

Lips,
mouth
eyes,
smiles
And a warmhearted feeling.
Such tenderness of your touch.
Melt me into the world of blue sky
and moonlight.
One perfect love never forgets.

THE FRESH AIR TO LOVE

———•———

Passion tingling and
Twirling on my mind like the
Fall I fell in and out of love
So quickly it left me nothing and feeling of lost
But I am transformed and fascinated by these beautiful
Birds that warm my heart beyond my horizon
And for once love through the lips,
shadowy façade and into
The part of me that loved Denver
I could close my eyes in touching your eyes
easily
But for once
I don't mind the fresh air flow into my face.

THE LOVELY FALL

That afternoon I feel cold,
in the windy fall of this year.
My happiness is grown
in beginning again.
Each day I write the romantic poem
For my love in the sweet dream, "missing him".
The fall is so marvelous:
The yellow moon on the dim sky,
autumn leaves fall down quietly.
The world of poems in the glass of wine
His soul drinks that glass of wine
Hold my body warm in his mind.
Like the rose is just bloomed
In the lovely fall.

MORNING SUMMER

As I sit there dreaming of the morning sunshine
heart beating with the teardrops on my face
I never know as you walk away that morning
silent of the moment and my soul remember dim
Everything was dared that morning,
never had the love of that summer
And my wait cried in the sunshine morning sky.
Watched the bird flied in sky,
To the soft hope for growth again.
But in my heart I hear the love song
As I admit my dream
That keeps me beating, over and again.

THE HIGH SCHOOL

To remember all of my friends and my Catholic teacher in Viet Nam
I missed my Gia-long high school
With my true friends in the white long-dress.
Waved me in the old dream
Of my childhood.
Time passed by fast,
It reminds me the best souvenir
that I never forget.
Oh, my goodness!
I want my youth age back.
It was so wonderful
With the great Catholic teacher
who tutored me:
Studied,
had fun,
loved parents,
loved country,
read the books
and lot of
Stories of different cultures.
(Had The Editor's choice's Award of year 2005)

SAIGON CITY

If you come back Saigon again
Please sent my missed love to the moon, the stars, and the forests.
Saigon where I was born in the warmth hands of my mom,
there were the rivers, the huge land of rice's, the deer's,
the lovers walked under sky of the nature's lovely way.
I love Saigon of the romantic afternoons,
the best friends waked me up the marvelous souvenirs
and the rains were never ending.
Oh, Saigon!
I love Saigon so much.
My life feeded me the sweet thoughts there.
The dreams of young age are existing in mine
Let me alive again for dreaming of the young age.
And the teardrops for my suffered country mixed in the raindrops.
To miss Saigon City—forever and always.

TEN

Screen door open a Country music song
Mama's wide eyes watch, clean the mess of my room
Ten years old that I knew all the poems of Nguyen Du, Ly Bach act . . .
Daddy called me "my little lovely girl"
in an accent thicker Chinese words
So gentle like Chinese songs
Lot of doctors loved my song of poems
In the vacant room at the top of his big house
We sat as party
On chairs
In the Orchid flower
And endured the music
I listened and enjoyed
Cleaned home make many things dreams
Broken bottle sliced my chair; I did not know
In the kitchen, mama used sugar for the coffee, and I
Delighted in Daddy's love offering
Honey tees hot in a cooler cup
From Uncle Wong's book store.

HIS ARMS

My love fills with joy
I do not know how to tell him
as he has captured me the love
and gleaming of my dream
I talk softly to him
As he touches me for the special moment
Along waiting the soft kiss
And dreaming of the moon stands still
As he holds me in his arms
That I have longed to make his mine
To share his sweetness openly
His arms are so warm and so forever
As he watches me starting erotic love
To dreaming of the world so blue
As he sustains to care and to save my life
My emotion deep stirs within his arms.

TEENAGER

He knew her when she was teenager.
The afternoon school breaks with dating.
"Purple" of missing . . .
Kiss her neck to feel her beauty:
Her deep black eyes, her laugh, her grace,
her more than just someone to him.
AS he thinks of her like the dream if life.
Now he is teenager.
He still loves her like the beginning
and dreams of her days and nights.
Together, they will be forever.

THE YOUNG GIRL, AN ANGEL FRIEND

I remember and I remember
down by the beach, where the water is blue.
My baby friend, I always think of her,
I remember the day, she went away
But my memories of her are with me to stay,
I remember and I remember
I look at the stars, her face I still see
I know she is here, still watching over me,
with this I know she is very near
but now I see that day very clear,
we were talking about our friends, in high school
She was leaning forward, and looking real cool,
I remember and I remember
from Mom and Dad's, we were just a few blocks
She went through the back garden.
The pavement beneath her, was blue and all stained
but now I know, she felt no pain,
we went through the young age, no one had seen
and she was so young, she was just twelve,
I remember and I remember that I wanted to play guitar,
by that very door

but she said no, and I fought no more,
she told me where I sat, safe I would be
that very day, she looked after me,
I remember and remember that it was a few days after,
she gave my belongings away
whoever would have guessed, she be an angel that day,
she is in a place now that has peace and love
She is up in the heaven's gate, in the sky above,
I remember and I remember
as I see the clouds, so puffy and white
I have this feeling, and now it feels right,
It's all because of her that I am still here.
Now I live my life, without any fear.
I remember and I remember as
I never knew that day, that I never would see her again
But she was more than just my best friends, but my angel friend.
My life that day, she really saved
It could have been me, lying in a grave,
I remember and I remember as she now has a halo, and a set of wings.
Also the toy she plays, I sing,
she became an angel friend, that very day.
And this feeling I keep, will never fade away,
I remember that I know one day, we will meet again
She is an angel friend, together happiness forever.

DOCTORS

To all of my doctors who saved my life with many thanks
My doctor likes an angel,
with beautiful eyes and mind.
A smile sweet, nice
and ready so sincere.
Sometime at daily route
My doctors saved people lives.
my doctors are all angels
Of God bring my life is getting well.
My doctors are the hearts of mankind and
a gift of God.
So loving and kind.
Through times passed by
among all of them.
They are my doctors of the miracle angels

MY INSPIRATIONAL POETS

Let me think of the Vietnamese literature
let me miss the poet named Ba Huyen Thanh Quan
Who is so lovely and so warm
As her romantic love poems are so clever and
forever for thousand years.
Let me dream of Nguyen Du
in the romantic love story of lady called Kieu
that is so fantastic love life
and the beautiful nature's lovely way
still lives in his poems forever.
Let my soul sinks in their marvelous poems
that are so simple and so beautiful for thousand years
As my childhood fills all of their poems
that let me stirs the emotion never forget.
To their beautiful poems are forever and always.

HANDSOME LOVER

Handsome lover, sing with me,
stars and blue sky are waiting for me;
Sounds of the song world heard whole day,
covering by the moonlight have all passed away!
Handsome lover, king of my life.
List while I sing the love song with soft melody;
Gone is the care of lovely life passed by
Handsome lover, sing with me!
Handsome lover, sing with me!
Handsome lover, out on the beach
On the lovely days come to end
Over the sea water vapors are bright
Waiting to see the blue sky and moonlight
Handsome lover, beam on my cold heart
Even the morn on the sand and sweater
Then will all clouds of sadness depart?
Handsome lover, sing with me!

AFTERNOON AUTUMN'S LOVE

When we walk through the colored leaves.
Our hearts become warm.
Your love wraps me up like the great sunshine.
With you, afternoon autumn
alives the sweet memories.
To the beautiful colored leaves
and stay in there for entire afternoon
to feel peace and true love
coming into our souls.
When you was kissing me.
I were watching the sky of the autumn
The dim moon under the sky of the
nature's lovely way
I thought of you as it kisses,
the whole day into evening.
With love, I will be yours forever.

WORLD NOW

Not handsome, nor the great love life
Of life, shall outlive this powerful melody;
But you shall shine more bright in these poems
Than sweet voice, sing the love poems.
When the terror war shall statues over the teardrop,
and human beings destroyed quick as well scenes,
tornado or hurricane made world in suffering
The September 11 in history with lost lives.
Death and all-oblivious terror everywhere
the lost life; the baby death and all destroy
Even in the eyes of all madness
That wear this world out of peace.
So, till the judgment that yourself arise,
You live in this, and teardrops in lovers' eyes.

HAPPINESS

Money is not the happiness.
Happiness can't sell or buy.
My happiness is my friends,
my lover and my family.
My happiness is charities,
It is supported by the people
Who cared about me?
It is also to help my mom
Recover her illness.
My happiness is my friends
At poet's workshop
That fills up full time to
read and review poems.
My happiness is to plant
The flowers
And to spent time
For my love's ones.
It is also my love
For my great country
That gives me a freedom
To think of the happiness,
an ordinary life and inspiration.

FEELING LOST

All day I have been written,
now I am tired.
I recall my memories: "When I will see you?"
But there is only the evergreen tree rustling in the rain.
The apartment is very quiet,
the sunshine in on my poems,
the orchid flowers and the tulips just on the table,
but you do not exist.
Suddenly I am lonely:
Where and I can see you?
I go about wandering.
Then I see you,
standing under the Christmas tree of the blue lights,
with the bright smile and your dozen roses on your arm.
You are cool, like silver,
and you smile.
I think the sunshine brighten you smile and behold me so warm.
You tell me nothing but in your eyes appear the warm heart.
Your mind almost burns beneath the blue skies
And I long remember all about us of my feeling lost
To see you have another girl in your arm

Made me want to crier and not want to see you again
Even a second in my love life
That makes me become colder heart than ever.

HER FAMILY

Another child, she remembers.
Another man, she loves
with her whole heart
full of love.
I found the pearls on her eyes.
Dreaming of her love and starlight
shadow of her husband.
With her eyes wide opened.
She read his letters
with great happiness.
Starting her love life so perfectly,
so self-fulfilling.
Her full love for him so wonderful
or is she dreamed of?

SECRET LOVE

Walking the long way in the bright light,
here my friends comes in the house,
I watch him pull and push the front door so heavy, brown, old,
new so lovely world, sound and songs are so marvelous.
We hands in hands, then kiss.
I feel his entire body-weight on my body,
his mouth is on my mouth, pulling me toward new life.
The gleaming of my dreams and he loves
with lot of the touch in our souls.
We become friendship in that lovely within the second.
The lovely time is gone with embrace and
continue like the delicious love.
When he is gone for several months.
His touch is still strong in mine.
My love desire is in me longer
from his love for me deep into the rainbow.
I must accept it like the soft love
that his soft hands, his black eyes,
the miracle of him, and of the heaven's gate itself,
making me fall in with him that he never knows
my secret love.

MY INSPIRATION

Blessing with the poets, an eternal joy,
who gave me spirits loves, and spirits cares,
the poets, who on world have made me inspires
Of truth and pure lobe by heavenly gate!
Honey be my name be poet among poet's world,
then happily would I end my desire days.

I TRAVELED WITH LOVE

Not as I since have loved him, as a desire
And surety of my eternal life, a light
Which I behold and feel he loves me
Nor his wish to so many words—
But for this love that I had seen him watch
His beauty in the morning love, had seen
The beautiful mountain at Denver touch his lovely soul
In many a thoughtful hour, when, from excess
Of happiness, my heart blood starts to beat
For its own pleasure, and I breathe with delight.

"SO MUCH WITHIN ME…"

Tear drops on my eyes, running
A joy to the happiness,
lost in a love of time,
and buried beneath the pool of discipline.
Hang over; hold on till all ceases,
as love, kiss and marvelous moments,
to cover the moon's gate,
and keep all of love life's secrets.

DEAR MOM

You've been in wheel chair so very long now
The pain inside me longer
So many words that I do say
But now the chance to see you without talk
All I ever want to make you proud
And for you to know how much I cared
But it seemed that we were just to want alive
And to say, "I love you" we just did not think of
We both keep our feelings buried deep inside
And never want what we want to say
So that now every day's a painful watch
And I blame myself for a chance to care my dearest mom
I should have told you thousand times that I loved you
And I should have kissed your face and should
Hugged you like a true loving daughter
Mom, whenever you are, if you're still on wheel chair
Know that I still miss you and I'll love you
Until I am no longer on the earth.

SOUVENIRS

And then I sat there
As if in a rain
Within the gentle breeze of but a few
Yet time just allow us joy
As every time you come so closer
That moment just seems to pass;
For every time you are nearby
Time just hold you till
When you dream seem to reality
Will you ever realize our true love?
How much my love would like to be
With you to let it settle.
Souvenirs may start a new
Moment of moments in time for all,
when I am forever holding you,
the sky is till blue as if we never do fall.
If the blue sky is going to hold till
The love within our hearts.
Then tomorrow you and I
Are forever—always

SPRINGTIME

The warmth Spring, soft touch my face
With bloom the flowers everywhere
The sunshine sparkles the sky
Watch the beautiful morning
Feel the trees of spring, so fresh
The morning Spring fills with joy
I dream of touching the moon.
Staying the sunshine.
Where I will call his soul
And the sweet moment spent with him.
The warmth breeze, whispered to my ears
With the happiness of sharing life together
Listen to the scene of the springtime
I'll dream of the perfect love
Till I give my life to him.

THAT SUMMER MOMENTS

As I sit there dreaming of the morning summer so perfect-
The times you hold me so close
To see in those beautiful blue skies- the gleam of all that dreams...
For the full—our loves never ending
To feel the rhythm of your heart and mine,
as our hearts beat in the perfect time
To feel you and me, as if by our souls-
Holding on that perfect time,
In our love captures of self to you only
That summer in time of self-me and you
Forever to you
My love I give.

WHEN SUMMER COMES

I will dress in blue skirt and silky blouse
Wear my new high shoes
Collared with green pearls
And silk blouse that sway like the
Oak
In August's honey-dewed winds
Dark, hot, the time is right
To change dresses.
The pearl one
Slides over my body
Like a silky desire
And when I dance tonight
At his wedding
The hot diamond strobe light
Will dance with me
Like the moonlight across my
Window in slow, white-diamond illuminated
In this season
Of red, red light
When summer comes.

08-15-2006

THE HEROES

This poem for the Veterans Day and my brother who died for freedom
Having no meaning of that night.
Let my mind forget in the sweet dream:
"I loved my country and friend
Who sacrificed for freedom.
In that dream, God let me wish, they all went to heaven.
Of course, they are the heroes."
Oh, my Goodness!
Once again,
May Lord God Bless America!
"The Heroes" is very special to me, as it commemorates to someone who was very important in my life "my brother was an officer Vietnamese Red Berets". His courage and strength has been inspirational to me. At the young age, he was the leader of the small group of soldiers. He died in the Vietnamese war before 1975 with honored. He graduated with honored at "Vo Bi Da Lat" and got the scholarship to study at US military but he skipped because he felled in love with the beautiful girl who studied at Gia Long High School and lot of his beautiful girlfriends at Dalat. He loved to become pilot a lot since he failed an eyes' exam. Then he joined to become

an officer Vietnamese Red Beret. His body cut half by stepping on the bomb because he did not want to bother the soldiers to check the bombs for him. He checked the bombs by himself. Now when I think about him. I am proud to be no exception. I enjoy writing poems for special occasions like The Veterans Day and as a gift to loved ones. Having the opportunity to tell my brother: "I love you", "May Lord God Bless Vietnamese Heroes!" and all the Americans soldiers who sacrificed for freedom in this poem is a beautiful way to share one's innermost feelings. I hope that others who have special people in their lives can relate to my love for my brother, and perhaps share my poem with their loved ones."

RED

Her hair is red
and brown,
slanted over her forehead,
it makes me laugh
and I sing.
She does not listen her music.
Just sings along with me
and lets her red roses all
over the floor.
Slipping, scratching, sinking
Her hands into my hands.
We sing together a few smiles
and listen she plays the guitar.

AT MOMENT

At moment, when all the spring bright
That warmed love life's early hour is come.
Your loving hands seek for mine
And hold them close at moment at moment!
We kiss at moment to dream
It's nest upon the leafless bough
By summer robbed, by winter chilled
By now, dear heart, you fall in love.
Though there are shadows on my naked body
And touch my cheek in truth.
The making lover where at moment we pleasure
Deep stir the joy of touching
Kissing at moment
Though fled is very girlish grace
Might win or hold a lover's moment,
despite my sad and faded face,
and warmed heart, you love me now!
I fear not all that moment or fate
May bring a joy heart of happiness-at moments- at moments...

DREAM

In infinity path we ran so quickly
Wandering on the forest
As the sunset is down
We breathe with fresh air,
ate with sorrow of sunshine,
reflected mirror in the shadow of moonlight,
and see the flowers are everywhere.
We continue the wonderful journey
of traveling through heaven's gate
and dreaming of the brightest future.

AUTUMN PLEASURE

Rolling warms soils of a red-orange
Spectrum leaves in with colorful
Dignity, the gentle arrival of a
Fall...
Changing weather blows gracefully through the fall,
carrying each to the beautiful season...
Trees rain swirling waves of color—
Quickly approaching their golden leaves
In the coming of
The breeze and silence of autumn...
The soft whisper of morning
Weaves its way across the land,
upon silhouettes of ancient shadows...
The grass sparkles with colorful
Leaves; heaven appears through
The dim skies, as the sunlight
Illuminates the delicate frost...
A rolling light rushes alongside a mountain,
carrying a fallen leaf over and through the rocks,
past the forests of pine, aspen, and maple...
Cascading over the waterfall-

The leaf takes one final flight
Upon elements of the wind and water.
Landing along a splendor of leaves
Floating atop a deep blue lake.
And all the fallen leaves on the ground, to one autumn pleasure.
Introduction:
When the fall comes. I think of the trees sparkle with colorful leaves,
The breeze and silence brings you the calm mind, the pleasure and
All the scenes that spread horizon. The fall bring you the love

GENERATION 6/13/2007

Each time I watch my mom.
I find myself draw in.
By the old dreams of my father life
And his father's before him.
I hardly image what my grandfather
Look like and what is on his brother's mind.
Even then I turned toward the imagination,
of my mind in a way that made me know.
He is no longer on this earth, to leave that set
Of love, that brown wrinkle skin on his face,
that gene he shared with our generations.
I am sincerely sure it reminds me of my daddy,
his relatives, his parent, me, my sibling
And all generation.
And the only place to look was in
Suffering love.

ONE MORE TIME

I walked through the shopping just to see your face.
I miss how the wind blow your hair,
The sunshine warm you as
You would not miss it away so carelessly.
I can still see your silhouette against the blue sky
The inky curvature that was your body,
So beauty, so perfect.
I used to want to feel the solidity of you.
I wrap myself around you
Wanting nothing more than these thoughts of you.
Holding onto a memory that is long gone
Buried in my lonely heart of hearts.
Now, as I hold on to a memory
Long ago and fading too fast,
I can almost feel you here.
Oh how I wish that I could be with you
How I wish for one more time.

THE DREAM COME ALONG WELL

As I think of my life
I kept telling myself
Love is suffering
When we first met
I promised you and myself
A life full of joy and happiness
As the days went and came
So many things went wrong
And I am to blame
You were there all the time
Loving, caring and by my side
So many days and nights
Happiness comes along
I promise you now
A heart full of life
A life full of love
A love dream full of joy
And the dream come along well!

HIM MY SUNSHINE

The sunshine has been up to many hours.
It's Sunday, and I feel fine on my fresh air.
Strong odor scents my living room.
He's breath smell sweet.
I am all excited for the day's sunshine to start.
I stand on the next to him and whisper his ears.
My living room is warm and friendly.
Today is a most special day and he knows why?
Sunshine is here, his bicycle
have been touched by the sunshine
He enjoys his mid-day with sunshine and blue sky.
After his afternoon bath with sunshine,
he looks at me with warm heart
My mind and my heart were pounding so fast.
He was so please to see me!
I thanked the fresh sunshine,
and he drove his bicycle in peaceful silence.
He, my sunshine, are my best friends,
always forever with me, you will be...!

CLOSED FRIENDS

Another friend is known
A true friend, I do love
To be with each other is such a joy
A piece of me is knows
Will I ever realize?-
A thought that never faked away.
You are my friend forever know
May we always have hope and ever be loved,
As we each other to see
For giving a new bright sunshine light,
And give me a new path to follow that seem ever right—
05-29-2007 @12:57

RIVER

Somewhere at river side
A driver who dives himself
on something other than the earth
touches his body to the surface
and lets it sink in,
no deeper than the thickness
of the sea.
And holds it firm,
his hand unwavering
as sunshine and blue skies spread all over,
office buildings, monuments
and falls like a blue ribbon from the earth,
and the river unanswered
itself, run down to the mountain
Spins

A FRIEND IS THE DESIRE OCEAN—

A friend is the Desire ocean
To see and to touch
To guide us, to behold us
To love us that much
The Desire ocean is strong
Bringing next to us daily
With wisdom, with kindness
Through triumph and melee
A friend is Buddha's helper
To help tend our needs
To soothe us and nurture
Most precious of seeds
And sometimes two Buddha
Unite and are friends
Flying in solitude
Till this life ends
A friend is The Desire Ocean
Who touches our being
Giving us vision
In all we are seeing
And if you are lucky

Your Buddha will know
A true friend in spirit
Will help you to grow

HER SONGS AT KEY WEST

———•◆•———

She sang beyond the deep sea,
the blue water never formed to her voice.
Like a body wholly mind, scattering
Its fullest love, and its motion
Made teardrops on eyes, caused constantly a cry,
that was not ours although we understood,
In human, of the Desire ocean
The sea was not a mask. No more was she.
The songs and water were our souls
Even if what she sang was what she loved,
since what she sang was uttered word by word.
It may be that in all her phrases stirred
The seawater and the strong wind;
But it was she and not the sea we listen.
For she was the writer of the song she sang.
The evergreen, beautiful blue sea
Was small a place, by which she loved to sing?
The evergreen, calm blue sea
Whose spirit is this? I said
If it was only the heavy voice of the blue sea
That tulips, or even colored by many waves;

However clear, it would have been deep air,
the heaving speed of air; a summer love
Repeated in a summer hot without end.
And melody sound lovely. But it was more than that,
more even than her gentle voice,
and our among the plunging of water and the breeze.
Theatrical distances, bronze shadows deep heaped
On high raindrops, mountainous of atmosphere heaped sky and sea.

NATURE

It is a marvelous evening, calm and free
Breathless with adoration, the broad sun
Is sinking down in its—tranquility-?
The gentleness of heaven's gate beyond the Desire ocean
Listen! The mighty being is awake,
and doth with his eternal motion make.
A voice likes wind—everlastingly.
Dear Child! Dear girl! That walks with me here,
If thou suddenly appear untouched by the solitude thought,
thy nature is not therefore less divine.

LOVE LIFE AS MY SOUL

I keep myself, and sing myself,
and what I accept you shall accept,
for everything belonging to me as good belong to you.
I hanging around and welcome your soul,
I waste and loafed at my ease observing a spear of summer love.
My tongue, every atom of my blood,
form's from the body, this fresh air,
born here of parents to become a soul, love to live,
I, now forty year olds in perfect health begin,
hoping to live not till death.
Creating the perfect life with perfect heart,
I think of myself many years and sing for the love never end . . .

A SUMMER DAY

Gently I stir my poem 's hat,
with open dress sitting
in an evergreen tree.
I take off my poem's hat
and hang it on an evergreen tree;
a wind from the trees
trickles on my hairs.

A SWEET KISS

I shall spend my love life in falling love,
teardrop by teardrop to fill this love
That seems my lonely soul.
And ache is alive,
not suffering past cries of empty heart.
But I have to know and feel in love,
all inspiration, embracing, and self fulfill,
securing my very worth to be love life
Yet shall I die with more than this?
My love life dying breeze, be as a sweet kiss.

TOMATOES

He used to leave the tomato, hot pepper
To dry on the windowsill, separated,
the largest on the left, diminishing in size
Until there was just a scrap of red left,
once dry, the tomato and pepper were so fragile
a strong gust of breeze could crack them.
He put them into soups, sauces and taste spicy
I remember his sunday sermons,
severe for a man who took such care
with the tomatoes and hot pepper.
But as we both grew older, and I learned
I realized the importance of tomatoes
Making order out of chaos,
Letting the juices dry,
keeping us all in line.
The juicy tomatoes make us
Remember the harvest day of grandma at South Vietnam

LONELINESS LOVE

From the hour I have not been
as others were; I have not thought
as others saw; I have not brought
my passions from a common summer.
From the desire source I have taken
my sorrow; I could live with
My heart to joy at the same love;
and all I loved, I loved alone.
Then- in my time, in the dawn
Of a most desire life- was drawn
From every depth of good and sickness
The mystery which binds me loveless:
From the torrent, or the fountain,
from the red cliff of the Desire mountain,
from the sun that round me love
In its autumn tint of well gold,
from the lightning in the blue sky
As it passed me flying by,
From the thunder and the tornado,
And the cloud that took the form
(When the rest of Heaven was pale blue)
Of a demon in my lineless.

STILL I LOVE

You may have me
with your bitter, twisted lies,
you may trod me in the very dirt
But still, like dust, I'll love.
Do my lovely eyes upset you?
Why are you beset with gloom?
'Cause I walk like I've got golden wells
pumping in my living room.
Just like moons and like suns,
with the certainty of tides,
just like hopes springing high,
still I'll love.
Did you want to see me die?
Bowed head and lowered eyes?
Shoulders falling down like teardrops.
Weakened by my soulful cries.
Does my haughtiness offend you?
Don't you take it awful hard
'Cause I laugh like I've got gold mines
Digging' in my own back yard.
You may shoot me with your own words,

You may cut me with your eyes,
you may kill me with your hatefulness,
but still, like star, I'll love.
Does my sexiness upset you?
Does it come as a surprise
that I dance like I've got diamonds
at the meeting of my thighs?
Out of the huts of history's shame
I love
up from a past that's rooted in pain
I love
I'm a blue ocean, leaping and wide.
Welling and swelling me bear in the tide.
Leaving behind nights of terror and fear
I love
into a daybreak that's wondrously clear
I love
bringing the gifts that my ancestors gave,
I am the star and the sorrow of the slave.
I love
I love
I love.

KISS OF MY DESIRE OCEAN

Your eyes overwhelm me
As you wrap your arms around me
I press your softness tight
Great love fills my well being
I'm captured in your soul
Your kiss control my very soul
The touch of your lips, heavenly
Forever love in time
keep me love you forever

A LOVE SONG

Once, at morning, in the Fall Wood
My friend and I long silent stood,
amazed that any rainbow could
Decree to part us, bitterly repining.
My friend, in aimless love and grief,
reached forth and sang aside a love song
that just above us played the love song
and stole our starlight that for us was unthinking.
A star that had remarked her love song
Shone straightway down that loved lane,
and wrought his image, mirror-plain,
within a tear that on her lash hung gleaming.
'Thus Time,' I laugh, 'is but a happy song
someone hath wept 'twixt hopes and fears,
yet in his little lucent sphere
our star of stars, happy alive song, is beaming.'

MISSING COLORS

Her white long-dress
make him like Daisy.
His blue shirt,
she loves her school.
Afraid love letters not enough
meaning of love,
he is fixing the purple pen
for missing colors.

AFTERNOON LOVE

———◆———

The lovely afternoon as I meet you
The bluebirds start to sing afternoon love song.
Flowers bloom everywhere of springtime's.
We walk through beautiful scenes of the blue afternoon,
the afternoon moonlight is so bright,
a gentle breeze stirs our desires,
and your eyes are so lovely and so warm.
I fall in love with you
for the special afternoon love in time.

AMANDA HARTLEY

For the moon are beams without bringing you dreams
Of the beautiful soul Amanda;
And the stars never rise but you feel the bright eyes
Of the beautiful soul Amanda;
And so, all the night-tide, you sit down by the side
Of my darling- my darling- your life and your daughter,
In the sepulcher there by the sea,
In her eyes by the sounding sea

AUTUMN AT VIRGINIA

She lives at Virginia, he lives at Tokyo.
Virginia's autumn leaves begin fall down.
Surprising, she lives at Virginia for a while.
But they never meet each other even once.
Watching the fall leaves, he thinks of spring.
Autumn's leaves begin fall down fast.
He is missing her lot likes the romantic spring at Tokyo.
She finds herself home sweet home at Virginia
And her lover is in her hands.
With joy and happiness
As she thought of the lovely fall
At Virginia
Together forever
They become one in the beautiful
Virginia's fall.

BROKEN HEART'

---◆---

I waited for half of my life to make him mine;
I nurtured him with my fullest love and raised him to love.
I saw him with another girl sitting to make love.
I wished him all the very best and felt everything should be fine and luck.

MISSING LOVE

I miss him when I reach his eyes.
I love him when I see his face.
I think of him when I wake up at mid-night.
And having sweet dreams each night of my life.

CONSCIOUS MIND

———•◆•———

Out of the night that make me conscious.
Black as the hole from place to place.
I thank whoever Buddha sees me
For my conscious soul.
In the fell clutch of circumstance
I have not known where I found cloudy.
Under the bludgeoning of chance
My head is hard, but conscious.
Beyond this heaven of wrath and tears
Looms but the horror of the shade,
and yet the menace of the years
conscious, and shall find, me unwilling.
It matters not how strait the gate,
how charged with punishments the scroll.
I am the master of my sorrow:
I am the river of my soul.

MOONLIGHT- HAIKU

The moonlight beyond dim skies,
stars are calm that night.
Nature stirs and sighs

MOM AND I

Wandering in the hallway.
Can't find happiness in the hospital.
Sick patients hoping to get well,
Confusing when and when mom's getting better?
Praying for her in the darkness night,
to wish her 's getting well.
Forever to Mom.
My fullest love, I give.

HIM...

I can never get my mind off him,
I wonder what his mind is if I'd,
make him as my lover,
and never let him go,
hug him tight,
care him right,
act all love,
he is taken me on a date,
make sure I'm never coming late,
kiss him on his lips,
talk about our desire future,
make him feel like king
living in a castle,
wish that is not too much hassle,
but I am so much in love
Wish I can be the lover,
hold him tight,
have my hand in his hand,
on my breast,
pass the words,
Now you're my man!

MOM AND BUDDHA

You are like the strong Desire ocean
What is the best that you can be my mom,
what really is worth as you are my mom?
What is love what is nice you are.
What is good cannot compare.
What I love for what I stand for your kindness,
Is full of passion it is not the sorrow as you can be,
and what I believe in is not half loss,
my buddha is real, mom should believe,
he is not one to be conceived,
he is mighty he is power,
he is one that no demon can devour,
he gave me strength as mom give me the life,
he is one that can only love
he only brings you up never down
he lifts you up off from that ground
my buddha is awesome and he lets me see.
That he is amazing and he is just for me and mom

I LOST MOM'S LOVE

Happiness, fullest love, desire inside as mom alive
My dreams have lost, my hopes have died as mom pass away
My mom love like more than Pacific ocean
Life's just passing with each season
She was my life, my hope, my love
All is gone, passed by thereof
The hurt is much such I should bear
What's to life, why should I care?
I weep all night for my love mom gone
My heart is sick, for death I long
Mine eyes well tears for love that's lost
I'll mourn always for the great cost
But in each day Buddha give me hope
Strengthen me so I may cope
Grant me wisdom to help me see
Thy great way and not just me as mom
Still and still exist in my mind.

www.ingramcontent.com/pod-product-compliance
Lightning Source LLC
LaVergne TN
LVHW020427080526
838202LV00055B/5055